7I0670062

ELIZABETH I

ELIZABETH I

ENGLISH RENAISSANCE QUEEN

by Mary K. Pratt

Content Consultant:
Katherine Scheil, associate professor of English
University of Minnesota

ABDO
Publishing Company

CREDITS

Published by ABDO Publishing Company, 8000 West 78th Street,
Edina, Minnesota 55439. Copyright © 2012 by Abdo Consulting
Group, Inc. International copyrights reserved in all countries. No
part of this book may be reproduced in any form without written
permission from the publisher. The Essential Library™ is a
trademark and logo of ABDO Publishing Company.

Printed in the United States of America,
North Mankato, Minnesota
062011
092011

♻ THIS BOOK CONTAINS AT LEAST 10% RECYCLED MATERIALS.

Editor: Mari Kesselring
Copy Editor: Rebecca Rowell
Cover Design: Kazuko Collins
Interior Design and Production: Marie Tupy

Library of Congress Cataloging-in-Publication Data
Pratt, Mary K.
  Elizabeth I : English Renaissance queen / by Mary K. Pratt.
     p. cm. -- (Essential lives)
  Includes bibliographical references and index.
  ISBN 978-1-61783-003-7
  1. Elizabeth I, Queen of England, 1533-1603--Juvenile
literature. 2. Great Britain--History--Elizabeth,
1558-1603--Juvenile literature. 3. Queens--Great Britain--
Biography--Juvenile literature. I. Title.
  DA355.P73 2012
  942.05'5092--dc22
  [B]
                                    2011013255

TABLE OF CONTENTS

Queen Elizabeth I

ELIZABETH
TAKES THE THRONE

It was January 15, 1559. Elizabeth, the only child of King Henry VIII and Queen Anne Boleyn, was just 25 years old. And, she was now England's new queen. Elizabeth had been preparing for this moment for a long time.

Elizabeth's older half sister, Mary, the previous queen, had died on the morning of November 17, 1558, after a long illness. Because Mary had no children, Elizabeth was next in line for the throne.

The people of England were divided along religious lines—some were Catholic and some were Protestant. Mary had been a Catholic ruler and had persecuted many Protestants who refused to convert to Catholicism during her reign. Although Elizabeth had converted to Catholicism during Mary's reign, she had been raised Protestant. Many Catholics viewed Elizabeth as a threat to Mary and their religion.

PROOF OF DEATH

Elizabeth learned about Mary's death within hours from members of the Privy Council, a group of advisers who help the king or queen make decisions. But the political

Bastard Status

Although Elizabeth was born while her father, Henry, was married to her mother, Anne Boleyn, Parliament in 1536 declared Elizabeth illegitimate and a bastard—terms applied to children born to unmarried parents. For Elizabeth, being named a bastard meant she was not a legitimate heir to the throne. However, Henry's will named her as third in line for the crown after his other children, Edward IV and Mary, so her status as a bastard did not block her ascent to the throne. Elizabeth and her councillors considered repealing the 1536 act at least once during her reign, but they never did.

events and religious upheaval happening in England at that time made Elizabeth suspicious. At the time, Elizabeth was staying outside of London, the capital city of England, at her estate in Hatfield. She refused to believe Mary was dead without evidence. She was afraid it was a trick. Elizabeth was convinced of her half sister's death only when Sir Nicholas Throckmorton brought her the engagement ring Mary had worn.

News of Mary's death and Elizabeth's ascension to power spread quickly. Parliament, the group of people who make England's laws, learned the news that same morning. The noblemen and elected commoners reacted to the news with a cheer of "God save Queen Elizabeth!"[1] The people of England celebrated, too. Churches in London jubilantly rang their bells. Residents abandoned their work to gather in the streets and cheer their new leader.

THE QUEEN TAKES ACTION

Elizabeth did not spend her first day as queen celebrating. Instead, she focused on choosing the men who would form her government. They would help her rule the country. She made her appointments quickly and decisively. Elizabeth made her Privy Council smaller than Mary's but nearly the same size as the council that had advised her father. There had been approximately 50 advisers in Mary's council. Elizabeth selected approximately 19 advisers.

One of Elizabeth's appointments was particularly notable. She appointed Sir William Cecil to the job of secretary. Elizabeth put all her trust in him, telling him "you will not be corrupted with any manner of gift . . . and will give me that counsel that you think best."[2] Elizabeth's trust was not misplaced. Cecil would go on to serve as her chief adviser for the next 40 years.

SEEKING SECURITY

Elizabeth's quick actions following Mary's death helped her solidify support as the new monarch, but her position and power were far from certain. Ceremony was a crucial part of government at that time. Mary had

Sir William Cecil

Sir William Cecil was one of the few people who remained a constant figure through most of Elizabeth's life. He most likely met Elizabeth when she was a teenager. The two shared an interest in learning and classical texts. For 40 years, Cecil kept careful notes as Elizabeth's secretary, and he provided guidance and advice.

William Cecil, Elizabeth's trusted adviser for most of her reign

to be buried. Elizabeth had to return to London to be crowned before she could fully assume the role and title of queen.

Elizabeth left Hatfield for London on November 23 with a procession of 1,000 lords, ladies, guards, and other advisers and supporters. She arrived in the capital on November 28, traveling along newly graveled streets that were decorated with tapestries once inside the city limits. Musicians and cheering residents greeted Elizabeth and her entourage. Elizabeth wore a purple velvet dress, the color symbolizing royalty.

Elizabeth stopped at the Tower of London, where she had been imprisoned four years prior when Mary suspected her of treason. Now, Elizabeth stayed in the tower, a home for well-connected political prisoners as well as free nobles and royals, as a resident for six days. She later moved to Somerset House, a palace in London, while waiting for Mary's final burial.

Mary's royal burial finally happened on December 13. Mary's

"I never thought to have come in here as a prisoner, and I pray you all bear me witness that I come in as no traitor but as true a woman to the Queen's Majesty as any as is now living."[3]
—*Elizabeth,
as she entered the Tower
on March 18, 1554,
on Queen Mary's orders*

coffin was then led on a procession through the city to Westminster Abbey, the burial place of many monarchs.

The Coronation

With one important ceremony done, Elizabeth turned her focus to the second ceremonial task: her coronation. On January 15, she would be crowned queen. However, the plans for the ceremony were not coming together easily. According to the country's rules, the archbishop of Canterbury was the religious leader charged with crowning England's monarchs. But the archbishop of Canterbury, Reginald Pole, had died the same day as Mary. The rules

Tower of London

The Tower of London dates back to the early 1080s, when William the Conqueror started building a massive stone tower as part of his fortress along the river Thames. Despite its name, the Tower of London is not really a tower. It is a monumental stone fortress that has served various purposes. English kings added on to the structure through the centuries. The royal family often ruled from it, as its size provided significant protection against enemies.

English monarchs used the tower not only as a fortress but also as a palace and a prison. The Tudor monarchs, including Henry, Mary, and Elizabeth, were particularly well known for their use of the tower to hold important political prisoners. Henry VIII imprisoned two of his six wives, Anne Boleyn and Catherine Howard, there as well as the writer Sir Thomas More. Although some areas were suitable for royal living, other parts of the tower were used for torturing and executing prisoners. The tower still stands today as a major tourist attraction.

also required the bishops of Durham and Bath to participate. However, the bishop of Durham, at age 84, was excused from Elizabeth's coronation due to his age. The bishop of Bath would not participate because of his loyalty to Mary's regime. Elizabeth's regime dismissed the possibility of using other bishops for her coronation because they supported Mary and the Catholic faith or had persecuted Protestants.

Elizabeth's Interest in Astrology

The English during Elizabeth's reign had a keen interest in astrology, or the belief that the positions of the planets and stars influence the lives and events happening on Earth. Elizabeth was no exception. She picked her coronation date, January 15, in part because well-known astrologer Dr. John Dee had suggested it as a favorable date.

After other leading bishops refused to help because of disagreements or illness from the influenza epidemic, a junior religious leader named Owen Oglethorpe, the bishop of Carlisle, agreed to officiate. And though more senior bishops had refused to officiate, most did attend the coronation, where they pledged their allegiance to their new ruler. Elizabeth, now Queen Elizabeth I of England, had finally reached the throne.

AN UNCERTAIN PATH

The peaceful transfer of power was dramatically different from the turmoil that surrounded

Elizabeth growing up and the religious and political turbulence swirling in England at the time. While Elizabeth did become queen without any bloodshed, her place on the throne was not fully secure.

Elizabeth inherited a country that was impoverished. England also had lost its standing among other European powers. The French had recently defeated the English in battle during Mary's reign. As a result, England had to turn over Calais, an important coastal region. Class divisions also plagued England, as the noble class and the rich often earned their wealth at the expense of the common people. The issue of religion continued to haunt England, with Catholics and Protestants battling against each other. At age 25, Elizabeth began her rule of a country whose future prosperity and security were far from certain.

"Be ye assured that I will be as good unto you as ever queen was to her people. . . . Persuade yourselves that for the safety and quietness of you all, I will not spare, if need be, to spend my blood."[4]

—*Elizabeth, speaking to commoners on the day of her coronation*

Elizabeth in her coronation robes

Henry VIII, father of Elizabeth I

THE UNINTENDED
MONARCH

rom the moment of her birth through much of her young adult life, Elizabeth's place in the English court was far from certain. Her parents, King Henry VIII and Anne Boleyn, his second wife, had expected a son who would be a clear heir to the throne. Instead, Elizabeth was born on September 7, 1533, at Greenwich Palace in London, England. Though the king and queen acknowledged their newborn daughter as a princess, many citizens of England questioned her legitimacy. They called her the daughter of "the great whore," believing Protestant Anne's marriage to the king had threatened to throw England into a civil war over religion.[1]

Elizabeth's troubles did not end there. The execution of Elizabeth's mother, Henry's subsequent marriages, his two other surviving children, and the scheming of the courtiers surrounding the royal family would threaten her status as princess and heir to the throne and endanger her life.

Henry VIII and Catherine of Aragon

The turmoil that surrounded Elizabeth's early years started well before her birth. Before marrying Elizabeth's mother, Henry had married Catherine of Aragon. Catherine was first married to Henry's older brother, Arthur, in 1501. Henry was only ten years old at the time. But Arthur died less than a year after the wedding. Henry married Catherine in 1509. He was 18, and she was 23. Henry's parents and Catherine's parents (the king and queen of Spain) had intended the marriage to create an alliance between the two countries. According to accounts from the era, the two young royals were willing participants in the union.

During her marriage to Henry, Catherine suffered a series of miscarriages. She had a son, born on January 1, 1511, but he died within days. Catherine also had a daughter, Mary, who was born on February 18, 1516.

The miscarriages took a physical toll on Catherine, who became overweight. English courtiers and subjects questioned whether she could even produce a son. Some suggested that God was punishing Catherine and Henry because they had gone against the Bible, which says a man should not marry his brother's wife.

Political and Religious Upheaval

The marriage between Henry and Catherine was not to last, however. Henry's patience for a son from Catherine had run short. At the same time, his love for another woman, Anne Boleyn, had grown. Anne was young, petite, and pretty, but she was not considered a beauty by the standards of the time.

Anne Boleyn

Though she was English, she had spent time in the
French royal court and had a French flair in her
mannerisms and dress. Anne came to the English

court as a lady-in-waiting, or assistant, to Catherine. Soon, Anne was openly flirting with Henry. Anne was willing to be the king's companion, but she made it clear the relationship could only proceed if he married her.

Smitten with the young Anne, Henry asked Pope Clement VII, the leader of the Catholic Church, to annul his marriage to Catherine—a move that would declare the marriage never existed. However, Catherine's nephew was Charles V. He was a powerful monarch in his own right, holding titles such as archduke of Austria and Holy Roman emperor. He made it clear that he would not allow the pope to annul the marriage. The stage was set for a religious rift that would change England—and the world.

In the early 1530s, Henry decided to take matters into his own hands. A group of clerics and academics supported him. They said Henry—not the pope—was both legally and historically the rightful head of the church. The English Parliament handled the details, passing laws that named Henry the supreme head on Earth of the Church of England. This gave Henry the opportunity to break away from the Catholic Church and establish a Protestant one in its place.

Now free of the pope's rule, Henry secretly married Anne on January 25, 1533, though still married to Catherine. Then, on May 23, 1533, Archbishop of Canterbury Thomas Cranmer annulled Henry's marriage to Catherine. On June 1, Anne was crowned queen. Elizabeth was born approximately three months later, on September 7, 1533.

Henry's desire for Anne and for a son put England and its royal court in turmoil. His actions created a civil and religious rift that would affect Elizabeth, her mother, and her siblings.

A Royal Upbringing

As an infant, Elizabeth was treated as a royal child. She was declared a princess and, as was customary, she was set up in her own home away from London and her parents. She lived in Hatfield, a country house approximately 20 miles (32 km)

"We are more bound to them that bringeth us up well than to our parents, for our parents do that which is natural for them—that is bringeth us into this world—but our bringers up are a cause to make us live well in it."[2]
—*Elizabeth*

north of the capital. Anne showered her daughter with fine clothes and accessories, though it would be months before Anne visited her daughter at Hatfield. Staff and servants essentially raised Elizabeth. She may have felt greater emotional ties to those who raised her than to her own parents.

There was another important figure in the young princess's household: her older half sister, Mary. As the firstborn legitimate child of Henry and his first wife, Catherine, Mary was first in line to the throne. But with the annulment of Henry's marriage to Catherine, Mary saw a dramatic change in her status. Once the marriage was annulled, she was considered a bastard child. As such, she could no longer hold the title of princess. Her rank was changed to lady, a change she and her mother refused to recognize. Additionally, the demotion in rank meant that Mary no longer had her own household. Mary was 17 years older than Elizabeth, but she was forced to move into her younger half sister's household.

Mary versus Elizabeth

Although Elizabeth was too young to understand the political issues surrounding her, these events would shape her ascent to power. Many in England, particularly Catholics, remained loyal to Catherine and Mary. These people detested Anne and Elizabeth, using coarse and slanderous language to describe them. They were ready to defend Catherine and Mary.

The tensions did not just involve the women and their daughters. Catherine and Mary remained devoted Catholics, while Anne embraced religious reform and the emerging Anglican faith, or Protestantism. Elizabeth was being raised in this new Protestant religion. So, citizens were not just divided by their loyalties to these women but usually by religion, too.

MORE MARRIAGES AND HEIRS

The annulment of Henry's first marriage to Catherine and his marriage to Anne had secured Elizabeth's place in the royal succession. However, that security was only temporary. Henry grew

Elizabeth's Education

Unlike most other women of her time, Elizabeth received a rigorous education. She had a series of tutors throughout her childhood, and they taught Elizabeth for hours each day. Elizabeth learned to write in the italic hand, which was considered a beautiful form of cursive handwriting. She also learned Greek and Latin, and she spent much time reading and translating the classic texts of ancient Greece and Rome. She also learned modern languages, including French and Italian. Elizabeth carried her interest in learning with her the rest of her life, and she returned to reading classic texts at the end of her life.

tired of Anne and angry at her assertiveness. He was also frustrated that she had not given birth to a son yet. Henry now wanted to marry another woman, Jane Seymour. But Henry did not seek to annul his second marriage. Instead, he charged Anne with adultery, had her arrested, and then beheaded. Anne's execution took place on May 19, 1536. Elizabeth, who was nearly three years old at that time, was too young to witness or understand what had happened. There is no record that she ever

---

Henry VIII's Six Wives

Besides Catherine of Aragon, Anne Boleyn, and Jane Seymour, Henry would have three additional wives. Henry's six marriages ended in different ways. One way to remember the fate of each one is this commonly taught rhyme: Divorced, beheaded, died, divorced, beheaded, survived.

Henry married his fourth wife, Anne of Cleves, on January 6, 1540. Anne was the sister of the Duke of Cleves, France. The marriage was an attempt to make the two countries allies. However, Anne did not fit well with the English court and tensions between the two countries were strained. Additionally, Henry did not find his new wife attractive and was already interested in another woman: Catherine Howard. Henry annulled his marriage to Anne of Cleves.

Sixteen day later, Henry married Catherine on July 28, 1540. However, rumors soon circulated that she was being unfaithful to her new husband. On February 13, 1542, Henry had his fifth wife beheaded.

Henry's sixth wife, Katherine Parr, had been married and widowed twice before marrying Henry on July 12, 1543. Katherine was widowed again when Henry died in January 1547. A few months later, she married Thomas Seymour, the younger brother of Henry's third wife, Jane Seymour.

spoke publicly or openly about her mother's execution.

After Anne's execution, Henry's marriage to Anne was ruled invalid. Henry married Jane on May 30. Jane gave birth to a baby boy, Edward, in October 1537, and died two weeks later. Anne's execution and Edward's birth created new uncertainties about Elizabeth's place in the royal family.

Though Edward, Elizabeth, and Mary lived together in one household while Edward was a boy, Henry's sordid marital life created problems when it came to succession. Edward, as a male, was clearly the first in line to the throne. Mary's and Elizabeth's birthrights did not seem to matter. England did not bar women from ruling, but since the king's marriages to the girls' mothers had been declared invalid, many questioned their legitimacy. In 1544, Henry and Parliament officially established a line of succession. Edward was first in line

Marriage Arrangements

Negotiations to marry Elizabeth started when she was a child and continued throughout her life. Henry considered marrying Elizabeth to the Earl of Arran, the son of the Scottish regent, although nothing substantial came of that idea. In 1544, Henry restored Elizabeth as an heir to his throne in his will, and interest in Elizabeth as a bride increased. Royal families throughout Europe and nobles within England proposed matches. Many negotiations followed, but they never led to marriage.

for the throne, followed by Mary, and then Elizabeth.

This action, however, was not enough to guarantee Elizabeth's security—or even her life—as she became a young woman. In fact, Elizabeth would face many struggles in the years ahead.

Female Leaders

While other countries, such as France, barred women from ruling during the Elizabethan era, England had no formal law against female royalty being part of the order of succession. Yet England had not had a woman successfully rule. The closest example until Mary's ascent to the throne was Empress Mathilda, who was never crowned but briefly held power in the twelfth century before the country began a civil war.

Elizabeth in her early teens

Elizabeth's younger half brother, Edward VI, was first in line to rule after Henry's death.

THE EARLY YEARS

Elizabeth grew up during an uncertain time in England's history. The country had been deeply divided over the issue of religion since Henry split from the Catholic Church and formed his own Protestant church (also called the Anglican church, or Church of England) in the early 1530s. Elizabeth was a witness to this division, historically known as the Reformation, throughout her young life.

Members of her family and the royal court also influenced Elizabeth. Katherine Parr, who became Henry's sixth wife in 1543, enthusiastically taught young Elizabeth, her stepdaughter, as a Protestant. She also helped continue Elizabeth's academic pursuits.

Elizabeth was also influenced by her half brother, Edward, who embraced Protestant beliefs. In 1547, Henry died and his son, now King Edward VI, succeeded him. Elizabeth followed Edward's lead, publicly worshipping in the Protestant faith.

Mary's Catholic Rule

Unlike Edward, Mary was still a devout Catholic. According to Henry's will, Mary was next in line for the

Violence during the Reformation

In 1517, Martin Luther nailed his "95 Theses" on a church door in Wittenberg, Germany. The theses exposed the corruption in the Catholic Church. Many others had pointed to these issues as well. The dissatisfaction with the church lead to the Reformation, which established Protestantism.

The Reformation created more than religious divisions in Europe. It brought about civil wars where neighbors fought each other because of their religions. Members of each side believed they were fighting for what God wanted, and that seemed to justify the cruel punishments inflicted on both sides. Kings, queens, and church leaders also fought for their religious beliefs, and they often resorted to brutal acts against those who did not believe in what they did. They tortured people and killed them in gruesome manners, such as burning them alive. Some victims were children.

throne after Edward, followed by Elizabeth. However, right before Edward died, at age 15 from tuberculosis in 1553, he named his cousin Lady Jane Grey as his successor. Jane's father, Henry Grey (the Duke of Suffolk) and John Dudley (the Duke of Northumberland and Jane's father-in-law) had convinced Edward to change the order of succession. Because Jane was Protestant, her rule would allow England to remain a Protestant country. However, most people, including Jane herself, felt Mary was the rightful heir.

Thomas Seymour

After Henry died on January 28, 1547, young Elizabeth was sent to different homes to live under the guardianship of various noble families. At one point, Elizabeth lived with her stepmother Katherine Parr, and Parr's new husband, Thomas Seymour. The arrangement proved nearly fatal for Elizabeth.

Seymour was an active and handsome man. Before marrying Parr, he had expressed interest in marrying the teenage Elizabeth. He did not hide his interest in Elizabeth while she lived with him either, though Parr was pregnant with their child. Seymour engaged in physical horseplay with Elizabeth, tickling her. Reports of the behavior badly damaged Elizabeth's reputation.

But Seymour's behavior toward Elizabeth's brother, Edward, was more troublesome. Seymour believed he should have been named the king's lord protector instead of his older brother who currently held the post. Seymour started to plot against Edward, but his plot was soon discovered. Seymour and other members of his household were imprisoned for treason.

Edward's men then turned to Elizabeth, taking her prisoner. They suspected she was part of Seymour's plans. Elizabeth denied plotting against her brother and was eventually released. Seymour, however, was executed in 1549.

Jane was not queen for long. Mary asserted her right to the throne, and the Privy Council decided to support her. After only nine days as queen, Jane was imprisoned. Some of the men who had plotted to place her on the throne were imprisoned or executed. Jane and her husband would eventually be executed in February 1554. Elizabeth had a clear example of the dangers she faced as next in line for the throne.

Mary was officially crowned queen on October 1, 1553. She declared Catholicism as the religion of the land. Mary wanted to end all Protestant practices. She condemned Protestants as heretics and traitors. Elizabeth survived under Mary by adopting Catholic practices, such as attending Mass and studying the Catholic faith.

To the Tower

Elizabeth became the focus of many plots to assassinate Mary and return England to Protestantism. This made Mary wary of her younger sister. In January 1554, Sir Thomas Wyatt led a rebellion against Mary.

Elizabeth's Hobbies

Elizabeth enjoyed many of the pastimes that were popular with others in the noble class. In her younger years, she particularly enjoyed riding horses and hunting. She also enjoyed dancing popular quick-paced dances. Elizabeth was considered quite good at these dances. In addition, Elizabeth liked music. She played the lute, a stringed instrument like a small guitar, and the virginals, a harpsichord-like keyboard popular in medieval and Renaissance Europe.

Mary was a Catholic queen.

He claimed he had written to Elizabeth regarding the rebellion. Elizabeth continually claimed her innocence and her devotion and loyalty to the

queen. Still, Mary imprisoned Elizabeth in the
Tower of London for two months. Afterward, Mary
continued to keep a close watch of her.

ELIZABETH RULES AS A PROTESTANT

Elizabeth survived Mary's rule and became queen
herself in 1558, following Mary's death. Despite
her conversion to Catholicism during Mary's rule,
upon her succession to the throne,
Elizabeth quickly established herself
as a Protestant monarch. Parliament
convened within two weeks of her
coronation and passed a bill that
abolished the supremacy of the pope.
It made Elizabeth supreme governor
of the Church of England, the
Protestant faith.

Parliament also established rules
regarding the practice of religion. As
queen, Elizabeth required obedience
to her laws regarding religion.
However, she showed a degree of
tolerance, particularly early in her
reign, toward those who disagreed
with her religious laws.

**History's Name
for Queen Mary**

Queen Mary's efforts to
restore Catholicism as
the state religion of England were collectively
referred to as the Counter-
Reformation. Mary's poli-
cies during her five-year
reign were often brutal
and violent. She ordered
hundreds of Protestants,
known as heretics, to be
burned at the stake for
refusing to follow the
Catholic faith. Her extreme
actions earned her the
nickname "Bloody Mary."

A MODERATE PATH

As queen, Elizabeth chose councillors who were Protestant and Catholic. Yet, her acceptance of people on both sides of the religious divide ironically earned her criticism from both. Some Catholic leaders considered her a heretic. Meanwhile, some Protestants felt she did not go far enough in ridding England of the papists—as Catholics were called because of their allegiance to the pope, their religious leader. One diplomat, Guzman de Silva, wrote about the situation:

> *The Queen is not popular or beloved, either by Catholics or heretics; the former do not like her because she is not a Catholic, and the others because she is not so furious and violent a heretic as they wish.*[1]

It was true that Elizabeth forged a middle ground. She combined some Protestant practices with the old Catholic ones. For example, she preferred English clergy to wear

John Foxe's
Book of Martyrs

John Foxe published one of the most important books of Elizabeth's reign in 1563. Foxe, a Protestant, left England for Switzerland when Mary came to power because he was afraid of persecution as a non-Catholic. He returned when Elizabeth took the throne and felt safe as a Protestant in England. He spent four years traveling throughout England collecting reports about the interrogations, trials, and executions of Protestants who were imprisoned during Mary's rule. He published these accounts in a book originally called *Actes and Monuments of these Latter and Perillous Dayes*, but the book quickly became known as the *Book of Martyrs*. Elizabeth used the book to build support for her Protestant church and ordered copies placed in every church.

vestments, the religious robes used by Catholic priests. Similarly, Elizabeth wanted English clergy to follow the practice of Catholic priests and remain unmarried.

Elizabeth was also more lenient when it came to enforcing mandatory attendance at English church services. Elizabeth attended the first celebration of the new English service, which was the first service using her reforms, on May 12, 1559. It was held just one month before people throughout England were required to use the Book of Common Prayer. This book gave instruction for performing different Protestant rituals, including prayer services, baptisms, and burials.

Although more moderate than her predecessors, Elizabeth did not intend to rule a country that allowed religious freedom. Elizabeth had decided to keep crucifixes and candles in her private chapels, which was a Catholic tradition. When the dean of St. Paul's Cathedral preached against this practice in 1565, Elizabeth interrupted the service, calling out "Leave that!"[2] She did not allow religious leaders to undermine her authority.

The city of London became a Protestant stronghold, and its residents embraced the Book

of Common Prayer requirement. English men and
women outside the city were not always so enthusiastic,
however. Many of them maintained their Catholic
faith. Elizabeth punished those who refused to
convert to Protestantism by taking away their offices.
She imprisoned them if they continued to refuse,
but she did not burn anyone, as her predecessor did.

Rifts Continue

Elizabeth's leniency and acceptance of some
Catholic preferences did not sit well with more extreme
Protestants. The growing numbers of Puritans, a
subsection of Protestants, were particularly critical
of Elizabeth and her lack of support for their beliefs.
Puritans wanted to rid the Protestant faith of any of
the remnants of Catholicism, which Elizabeth had
incorporated into the Church of England in order
to appease the Catholics.

Although Elizabeth brought a measure of
uniformity to religious practice in England, her
tolerance during the early years of her reign would
yield to a harsher stance later in her life. She would
sometimes severely deal with both Catholics and
Protestants who disagreed with her positions on
theology and church hierarchy.

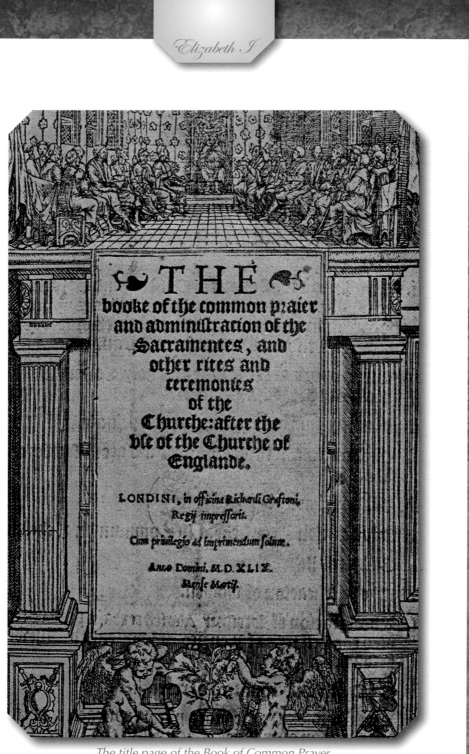

The title page of the Book of Common Prayer

*Elizabeth's advisers wanted her to marry
so that she could produce an heir to the throne.*

THE VIRGIN QUEEN

After taking the throne, Elizabeth's marriage prospects became a matter of public interest as well as courtly gossip. Near the start of Elizabeth's reign, members of the House of Commons, the lower chamber of Parliament, asked the queen to marry and start a family. That way, Elizabeth could give the country an heir to the throne. Elizabeth did not feel the same sense of urgency to marry, declaring in 1559, "In the end, this shall be for me sufficient, that a marble stone shall declare that a Queen, having reigned such a time lived and died a virgin."[1]

Despite such statements, English leaders spent a good deal of time trying to find a suitable husband for Elizabeth. Because she was both a member of the royal family and an heir to the English throne, her marriage was a matter of state affairs. A good match could help England by creating new allies and strengthening existing friendships with other countries. It could bolster the royal family's position among other important English families. A bad match could create problems by alienating other monarchs and deepening the religious divisions. It could even threaten the stability of the English crown.

SUITORS CONTINUE

Parliament needed to approve any match, since marriage was not about love but, rather, primarily about political and religious strategy. Elizabeth recognized that, and she often considered matches for possible political gain. But she also realized that she was pretty, something that helped her attract potential husbands.

On the other hand, Elizabeth received many proposals that she rejected. In 1554, on learning that the Swedish king had asked that Elizabeth marry his son, Prince Eric, Elizabeth had written to Queen Mary, telling her that she did not wish to marry. When talking about marriage, Elizabeth often asserted that she was opposed to it. In 1563, Elizabeth

Elizabeth on Being a Woman

Elizabeth's life was extraordinary for many reasons, including the fact that she was able to command so much power at a time when women were seen as inferior to men. Elizabeth often referred to her gender, and some of her statements hint that she, too, believed women were the weaker sex. However, it is difficult to know for sure how Elizabeth felt about women.

Some of her comments also show that she had a sense of humor about the issue. She once responded to a Frenchman who commented on her ability to speak six languages besides English by saying, "It is no marvel to teach a woman to talk. It were far harder to teach her to hold her tongue."[2]

During the Elizabethan era, women could not hold any public office, but, as Elizabeth proved, they could rule as queen. Most people accepted this because they believed in the divine right of royals. That is, they believed God had chosen them—whether they were male or female—to rule. But not everyone agreed with this viewpoint. In his 1558 book *The First Blast of the Trumpet against the Monstrous Regiment of Women*, John Knox addressed the issues of female monarchs. Knox, a Protestant, said in his book that God did not intend women to rule, so no one should obey a woman ruler.

supposedly said she would be a "beggar woman and single, far rather than queen and married."[3]

Robert Dudley

Elizabeth did fall in love with a few men during her life. She developed a deep affection for the handsome Lord Robert Dudley during her early reign. Elizabeth and Dudley were only months apart in age and had known each other since they were children. In 1558, Elizabeth made him master of the horse, an important and respected office within her court.

Despite evidence that Elizabeth and Dudley had shared a strong romantic attraction, Dudley was already married. He had wed Amy Robsart, an heiress, in 1550, when he was 17. But Robsart became seriously ill by the decade's end. There was speculation that her death would leave Dudley free to marry Elizabeth.

Elizabeth's Style

As a young woman, Elizabeth was considered attractive. She had the fair hair, fair skin, and high forehead considered beautiful during that era. She dressed in modest clothes of muted colors when younger, but she wore striking colors such as red and yellow when she was an adult. Later, she often wore black and white. She also had jewels and pearls sewn into her clothes. Elizabeth was conscious of her appearance and of the power of her beauty. She was proud of her beautiful hands and long fingers, which she liked to show off. However, she did not like to sit for portraits. And she did not like the portraits that were sold to commoners; she found them low-quality paintings and ordered them destroyed whenever found.

Robsart, however, did not die from an illness. Rather, she died from a fall down some stairs in 1560. Elizabeth's courtiers considered the death—and Dudley—suspicious. The scandal surrounding Robsart's death made it nearly impossible for Elizabeth to take Dudley as her husband even though he was now available to marry.

Still, Elizabeth and Dudley were rumored to be lovers for decades. Elizabeth continued to support him with appointments and titles. She made him Earl of Leicester in 1564. However, she never married him.

TROUBLE TO THE NORTH

Meanwhile, Elizabeth was occupied by foreign affairs that would affect the rest of her reign. She was constantly vigilant against foreign threats, particularly from Spain and other Catholic countries in Europe. Similarly, Elizabeth watched for

The Virgin Queen?

Elizabeth has often been called the Virgin Queen, but the name may not be accurate. True, Elizabeth never married. But she had close relationships with many men. There were also rumors that Elizabeth had had children without being married. Even though there was no evidence of illegitimate children, these rumors spread through England and to other countries, hurting Elizabeth's reputation among her subjects and other rulers.

Sir Robert Dudley

opportunities to advance England's interests abroad and increase its dominion over other countries. The fact that foreign leaders were often related to each other and could claim other rulers' thrones complicated these thorny matters. Animosity between Catholics and Protestants also played a role in Elizabeth's decisions about foreign affairs. She was often swayed for or against action in other countries based on religion.

Much of Elizabeth's foreign troubles came from Scotland. Ruled by Catholic monarchs, Scotland, like other European countries of the era, was being torn apart by religious divisions. Mary Queen of Scots was the Catholic queen of Scotland during Elizabeth's reign. Mary was the granddaughter of Henry VIII's older sister. Therefore, some Catholics hoped she could replace Elizabeth as queen of England.

MARY QUEEN OF SCOTS

Mary Queen of Scots was Catholic. Her father, King James V of Scotland, died six days after Mary's birth in 1542, making Mary Scotland's queen. Mary's mother, Mary of Guise, became queen regent of Scotland. A regent serves when a king or queen is still living but cannot rule usually due to age or illness. Meanwhile, Mary Queen of Scots was educated in France from ages five to 18.

In May 1559, John Knox and a Protestant group called the Congregation led the charge against Mary of Guise. She called on French troops to help quell the Congregation, who were sacking abbeys and destroying Catholic images throughout Scotland. The thought of French troops in Scotland was particularly worrisome to Elizabeth because France at the time was engaged in its own religious strife. In France, the ruling Catholics, led by the Duke of Guise, were brutally persecuting Protestants.

Elizabeth believed in the rights of ruling monarchs and, under different conditions, might have supported Mary Queen of Scots and her regent against the Congregation. But Elizabeth was angry that Mary Queen of Scots had made claims to the English throne in 1558. Plus, Elizabeth saw the strategic advantage of an English victory over Scotland.

Elizabeth and Her Ladies

Elizabeth was surrounded by a number of ladies and maids in waiting, but their relationships were often far from friendly. The women around the queen gossiped about her and sometimes sold secrets about Elizabeth and her court to foreign diplomats. The queen could be cruel to her women, though, and often expressed her anger to them. She would also deny them the right to marry if she felt the match was not suitable, even if the couple wanted to wed.

England Steps In

Sir William Cecil, who was one of Elizabeth's leading advisers, further swayed her to take action to help the Protestant Congregation. He argued that the Congregation was not a band of traitors and rebels to Mary. Cecil claimed the Congregation was fighting against the regent's decision to bring in French troops. Elizabeth gave her support to the Congregation. She backed diplomatic efforts and gave the Scottish Protestants money to pay for their cause. In December 1559, Elizabeth sent English soldiers to help the Congregation.

In June 1560, Mary of Guise died. Mary Queen of Scots returned from France and began ruling Scotland on her own. Meanwhile, the English-backed Congregation was victorious. Elizabeth's maneuvers meant the end of French troops in Scotland. The Treaty of Edinburgh was signed on July 6, 1560. It represented a significant victory for Elizabeth and the Congregation, who established a Protestant state in Scotland. However, it was not the last time Elizabeth would hear of Mary Queen of Scots.

Mary Queen of Scots

Elizabeth on her throne at Parliament

CHALLENGES
TO HER RULE

From an early age, Elizabeth saw that even monarchs were not safe from slander and death. Her own mother was beheaded. She and her half sister, Mary, were at times outcasts from the royal court and their lives were often in danger.

When Mary ascended to the throne, Elizabeth believed the queen was planning to execute her. Even as queen, Elizabeth was not out of harm's way. Some subjects continued to question her claim to the throne, saying that as the daughter of Henry's second marriage, she was an illegitimate child and therefore was ineligible to rule.

Elizabeth survived assassination attempts and plots against her throughout her reign. There were frequent rumors that foreigners managed to make their way into her court with the intent of poisoning Elizabeth. Catholics abroad urged English Catholics not to obey her. Some Catholics, who hoped to assassinate Elizabeth and make Mary Queen of Scots the new queen, formulated many plots against Elizabeth's life.

CONTINUED THREATS FROM THE NORTH

Mary Queen of Scots posed a particularly significant challenge to Elizabeth's rule. After the Treaty of Edinburgh, Scotland became a Protestant state. Mary herself remained Catholic. Elizabeth and her advisers still feared a religious war in Scotland. Such a war could lead to religious troubles in England too.

Mary's religion was not the only problem with the Scottish queen. Mary recognized Elizabeth as the lawful Queen of England, but Mary was also considered an heir to the English throne. Mary asked Elizabeth to acknowledge her as Elizabeth's successor. Mary told Elizabeth that honoring that request would create a friendship between the two rulers.

But Elizabeth always refused to name a successor. She was afraid that any successor might try to depose her in order to claim the English throne. Elizabeth stayed true to form and refused Mary's request. Elizabeth declared, "Ye think that this device of yours should make friendship between us, and I fear that it should produce the contrary effect."[1]

The two monarchs tried to arrange a meeting during the first several years of the 1560s, but they were unable to make such a large diplomatic undertaking work. Soon

"I know the inconstancy of the people of England, how they ever mislike the present government and have their eyes fixed upon that person that is next to succeed."[2]

—*Elizabeth to Mary Queen of Scots's secretary of state*

England became involved in the French Civil War. Elizabeth's advisers warned her against meeting with the Catholic Mary while England supported the Protestant Huguenots in France. So, Elizabeth postponed several proposed meetings with Mary.

THE FRENCH CIVIL WAR

Elizabeth had become an influential and powerful ruler during the 1560s. Her success in Scotland with the 1560 Treaty of Edinburgh encouraged other foreign Protestants,

Containing Threats to Her Rule

Elizabeth never believed her position as queen was completely secure. She often took action against those who might overthrow her. That was the case with Katherine Grey. Katherine's father and older sister, Jane, had been executed for treason during Mary's reign. Elizabeth may have worried that the other Grey daughters would seek to take the throne. She kept Katherine and her younger sister, Mary, at court, probably so she could keep an eye on them.

Katherine wanted to marry a man named Edward Seymour, Earl of Hertford. The Act of 1536 required members of the royal family to get the monarch's consent before marrying. Elizabeth refused to grant permission to the couple. Historians believe Elizabeth thought her opponents might make Katherine queen if Katherine married and had children.

Katherine and Seymour secretly wed. Elizabeth learned in 1561 that Katherine was pregnant and had the couple locked in the Tower of London. Elizabeth declared that no marriage took place and therefore their child, a boy, was illegitimate. Jailers at the tower allowed Katherine and Seymour to live together while in prison. Katherine gave birth to another son in 1563. After that, Elizabeth had Katherine moved from the tower and placed under house arrest until her death in 1568. Seymour was freed after Katherine's death.

*Protestants and Catholics fought against each other
in France's bitter civil war.*

who saw it as a sign that they could defeat the
Catholic rulers who had persecuted them. Elizabeth
supported the Protestant cause. In fact, in 1561,
Elizabeth sent an ambassador, the Earl of Bedford,
to France to persuade the French monarchy to make
France a Protestant country.

In the 1560s, France was having a civil war over religion. Catholics were massacring Protestants and Protestants were retaliating. Elizabeth sent 6,000 soldiers to France to aid the Protestants, and she loaned the Protestant leaders money. The Catholics and Protestants in France demonstrated remarkable brutality in their fighting.

THE QUEEN IS ILL

As England intervened in the French Civil War, Elizabeth was fighting a more personal battle. In October 1562, the queen contracted smallpox, a terrible disease that killed many and left bad scars on those who survived. Elizabeth was close to death for several days.

Elizabeth had not yet named a successor, so her advisers were afraid the country would break down into turmoil if the queen died. They also worried that whoever did take the throne might turn the country back to Catholicism, which could mean more fighting and executions over religion. They also feared what would happen to English interests in France if the queen died. Fortunately, Elizabeth started to recover several days after being diagnosed and survived without severe pox marks.

A Loss for the Protestants

Despite the English Protestant troops in France, the Catholics were the stronger force. By 1563, the Catholics were winning the French Civil War. Elizabeth was forced to evacuate the surviving 3,500 English troops from the French city of Le Havre.

Elizabeth's defeat in France had far-reaching consequences. Protestants across Europe were demoralized by the events. Elizabeth herself decided she would no longer champion the Protestant cause abroad, though she did give some limited support to Protestants in later battles. Elizabeth's intervention also cost England the French coastal town of Calais. The French were expected to return Calais to England in 1567 based on a treaty, but French rulers determined that Elizabeth's intervention in their civil war violated the treaty and refused to give Calais to England.

Defeated Soldiers Bring the Plague

The English loss to the French in the French Civil War was a significant defeat for Elizabeth, but the battle did not end when her soldiers were forced out of Le Havre. Many of the English soldiers in Le Havre were sick from the plague, and they brought the plague to England when they returned home.

CONTINUED PRESSURE TO MARRY

Meanwhile, members of Parliament, as well as Elizabeth's councillors, were still eager for her to marry. They wanted Elizabeth to marry to create strategic alliances and to have a child who could become the ruler upon her death. Councillors and ambassadors suggested unions with other rulers, including Charles IX of France, who was 17 years younger than Elizabeth, and Archduke Charles of Austria, another European royal. But Elizabeth, for the most part, resisted their efforts to find a match.

In 1566, Elizabeth became angry when Parliament refused to give her the supplies she wanted until she discussed the issue of marriage with them. Elizabeth, who almost always displayed her strong will as a ruler, believed Parliament was overstepping its authority and meddling too much in her affairs. Many officials worried that, without an heir, England

"The weight and greatness of this matter might cause in me, being a woman wanting both wit and memory, some fear to speak, and bashfulness besides, a thing appropriate to my sex. But yet, the princely seat and kingly throne wherein God (though unworthy) hath constituted me, maketh these two causes to seem little in mine eyes."[3]

—Elizabeth's defiant reply to Parliament, which in 1563 asked her to name a successor and introduce legislation to make her plans for succession a law would be thrown into turmoil when Elizabeth died. However, Elizabeth continued to assert that she would never marry and refused to name her successor. And she would remain true to her word.

Charles IX of France was one of Elizabeth's many suitors.

Mary Queen of Scots married Henry Stuart, the Earl of Darnley, in 1565.

GROWING POWER

Elizabeth's defeat in France would influence her future decisions regarding English intervention in the name of the Protestant faith. She became more hesitant to become involved in other countries' affairs. Elizabeth was also reluctant to intervene in Scotland as Mary Queen of Scots's rule in that country became increasingly unstable.

TROUBLE WITH SCOTLAND

Even as the French Civil War came to an end, Elizabeth was still concerned about Mary Queen of Scots, who threatened her rule. Elizabeth tried to arrange a marriage for Mary, suggesting at one point that Mary wed Elizabeth's own longtime love interest, Robert Dudley. Historians think Elizabeth proposed the union because she knew Dudley could keep Mary friendly to Elizabeth and to England. Mary decided instead to marry Henry Stuart, the Earl of Darnley. They were married in 1565.

Scotland at the time was poor and prone to lawlessness. That trouble infiltrated Mary's court. Mary's husband, Stuart, was unfaithful, troublesome, and unpopular. Mary

Elizabeth's Fears

Elizabeth's constant need to protect herself took its toll. She would sometimes alter the routes of processions at the last minute to help protect her from potential attacks. In 1579, she told the lord mayor of London to keep large crowds from gathering when she rode over London Bridge on a planned procession. She sent another message telling him to make sure those who did gather were not armed. Then, she sent a third message saying she had changed her mind and would not be going over London Bridge at all.

herself was having an affair with James Hepburn, the Earl of Bothwell. When Stuart was murdered on February 9, 1567, Hepburn was accused of the crime. Hepburn and Mary were married shortly afterward. Although Mary later stated that she married Hepburn against her will, these sordid events made Mary unpopular. There were rumors that Mary had helped plan Stuart's death. The Scottish lords arrested her on June 15, 1567, and sent her to prison. Hepburn eventually died in prison.

A Monarch's Right to Rule

Elizabeth did not support Mary Queen of Scots, but she did not believe that the Scottish people had the right to remove her from her throne, either. Elizabeth believed God ordained monarchs to rule. She told her advisers that the Bible states that subjects should obey their rulers. She felt that those who were rebelling against Mary were going against God.

In 1567, speaking on the issue of Mary being called to answer to the lords of Scotland, Elizabeth told an adviser that:

> We think it is not lawful nor tolerable for them, being by God's ordinance subjects, to call her, who also by God's ordinance is their superior and Prince, to answer to their accusations by way of force, for we do not think it consonant in nature the head should be subject to the foot.[1]

ELIZABETH RESPONDS TO MARY'S ARREST

Elizabeth did not like Mary's actions, but she believed in the monarch's right to rule. Elizabeth reacted to Mary's arrest by threatening to wage war against the Scots. She wanted to restore Mary to the Scottish throne. But Mary, while in prison and under threats from the Scottish lords, agreed to abdicate, or give up, her throne.

On July 29, 1567, Mary's 13-month-old son, James, became King James VI of Scotland. Mary escaped from prison in 1568 and her Scottish army tried to retake the throne by force. However, Mary's army lost, and she fled to England. Once she was in England, Elizabeth worried that Mary would try to take the English throne. Elizabeth imprisoned Mary. For the time being, Elizabeth had control of the situation.

The Northern Rebellion of 1569

Despite her experience with the French Civil War, Elizabeth did not completely avoid international confrontations and diplomatic strategies. She continued to maintain a strong grasp of the importance of international relationships and diplomacy. She was more than willing to take up arms and support specific causes if she saw a clear benefit for England and for herself as its ruler.

The religious changes that Elizabeth had enacted during her first ten years as queen had firmly established Protestantism in much of the country.

Mary Queen of Scots arrived in England and became Elizabeth's prisoner.

Many of the English people who remained Catholic were loyal to her, too. But Catholics in northern parts of England remained opposed to Elizabeth and her Protestant councillors. The Catholic Earls of Northumberland and Westmoreland, two counties near the border with Scotland, plotted a rebellion against Elizabeth in the winter of 1569 and 1570. They wanted to restore Catholicism as the state religion and place Mary Queen of Scots on the English throne.

Elizabeth and her advisers learned about the planned uprising before it started. She had several leaders arrested and imprisoned, but the rebellion continued. Rebel Catholic forces marched into the city of Durham on November 14, 1569. They burned the English Bible and Book of Common Prayer and celebrated the Catholic Mass at Durham Cathedral.

Elizabeth raised her own army of 28,000 men and placed them under the command of the Earl of Sussex. He drove the rebels across the Scottish border within six weeks.

Excommunication of Elizabeth

In 1570, Pope Pius V excommunicated Elizabeth from the Catholic Church, which meant she was barred from being part of the Catholic community. During Elizabeth's time, Catholics believed excommunication would damn someone for eternity. The pope's words also threatened to rouse some of Elizabeth's citizens against her. The pope declared that "peers, subjects and people of the said Kingdom and all others upon what terms so ever bound unto her are freed from their oath and all manner of duty, fidelity and obedience. . . . They shall not dare to obey her or any of her laws directions or commands."[2]

He executed poor rebels and left bodies hanging in villages and along roads as a warning to others who opposed the queen's beliefs. He allowed wealthier rebels to live, but he confiscated their properties. Elizabeth did not immediately condemn Mary Queen of Scots to death, despite her support of the rebels. Mary languished under arrest for several years.

An International Match

Meanwhile, Elizabeth continued to use her unmarried status as a diplomatic tool. She held out the prospect of marriage to other rulers as a way to create new alliances or strengthen existing alliances between England and other countries. But she had to be careful about the religion of potential suitors. Catholics were afraid that if Elizabeth married another Protestant, they could face increased persecution. And Protestants worried that a Catholic husband could mean Elizabeth's conversion to that faith and a renewed persecution of Protestants. The English people were not the only ones concerned about the religion of Elizabeth's suitors. Many European countries were divided over religion. Throughout the continent, people of all ranks, from monarchs to commoners, worried about the religious consequences if Elizabeth finally married.

Many of these factors were evident in 1579 when Elizabeth started negotiating marriage with François, Duke of Alençon, the younger brother of King Henry III of France, whom she had never met. Elizabeth was 45, long past the usual age for women to have children during that era, but doctors assured her and her advisers that she could still safely have children. So negotiations continued through the early part of that year. Elizabeth told those around her that a royal wedding would soon take place, but some questioned whether it would really happen. François was short and rather unattractive. At 25 years old, he was much younger than Elizabeth. He was also Catholic. Many in Elizabeth's court wondered if the couple would make a good match.

François, Duke of Alençon

François was born on March 18, 1554, in France. He was the youngest child of the king of France, Henry II, and his wife, Catherine de Médici. François had three older brothers—Francis II, Charles IX, and Henry III. Henry had also once been a match for Elizabeth. However, she had rejected him. François's brothers all had reigns as kings of France. François also would have ruled, but he died at the early age of 30.

Elizabeth and François finally met on August 17, 1579, when he traveled to England for a visit. They became quite fond of each other. Still, many of Elizabeth's advisers were opposed to the union. Dudley was jealous. Many English citizens also opposed Elizabeth's marriage to François.

Negotiations for a marriage continued for three years. But Elizabeth's affection for François wore off as he made demands for money and entitlements. Elizabeth had her own demands, and French royals grew tired of them. For example, she wanted the city of Calais returned to English control. François left England in February 1582 and never returned.

Elizabeth continued to be courted by men. Some may have actually been in love with her. She also stayed close to Dudley. But suitors were not all Elizabeth had to deal with as she entered the twilight years of her reign. More religious upheaval moved Elizabeth to respond in a harsher fashion than she had in previous conflicts. ⌒

François, Duke of Alençon

Elizabeth was often seen by the rest of Europe as the center of the Protestant faith.

CONFLICTS
at HOME AND ABROAD

The Elizabethan era was far from peaceful. The power struggles between Catholics and Protestants and between the various rulers throughout Europe kept Elizabeth constantly working. She had to guide her country through delicate diplomatic situations abroad as well as challenges at home. However, not everyone was happy with the way Elizabeth ruled the country.

Elizabeth's reputation was beginning to suffer by the middle part of her reign. She swore frequently and was often ill-tempered and abusive to those around her. And her liaisons with men, including a courtier named Christopher Hatton, fueled rumors about her poor behavior. Meanwhile, squabbles with other countries continued, dragging England into religious and civil strife elsewhere and draining money from the country's reserves.

PURITANS AND DUTCH ANABAPTISTS

Although Elizabeth exhibited leniency during the early part of her reign, she tightened her grip on religious practices as her monarchy progressed. The Puritans and the

A Reputation for Swearing

One Puritan sent Elizabeth a note that chastised her for her bawdy and often blasphemous language. He wrote, "By your majesty's evil example and sufferance, the most part of your subjects and people of every degree, do commonly swear and blaspheme, to God's unspeakable dishonor, without any punishment."[1]

Dutch Anabaptists, who were considered more radical Protestants because of their beliefs, were problematic for Elizabeth. They defied English law by practicing their faith, but the only religion Elizabeth allowed was that preached by her own Protestant English church. During the 1570s, the Puritans became increasingly bold in their criticism of Elizabeth, who engaged in the lively pastimes and frequent swearing that the Puritans disdained. Puritans publicly spoke against the queen, too, sometimes being so bold as to criticize her in Parliament and from the church pulpit.

Although the Puritans saw Elizabeth as a Protestant figurehead who was an ally against the pope and Catholicism, their actions made Elizabeth angry. She was more religiously moderate than the Puritans, so she sought to end the spread of their faith. She ordered her church's leader, the archbishop of Canterbury, Edmund Grindal, to put an end to the Puritans' practice of prophesying, but he refused because he felt the practice was spiritually good. He even gave Elizabeth a warning: "Remember Madam that you are a mortal creature, and although ye are a mighty prince, yet remember that he which dwelleth in heaven is mightier."[2]

Still, Elizabeth was open in her dislike of the Puritans. In 1575, she allowed two Anabaptists convicted as heretics to be burned alive at the stake as punishment. Elizabeth's predecessor had allowed this punishment against convicted Protestants, and the English came to associate it with Queen Mary and other Catholics. But this was the first time Elizabeth had ordered this extreme punishment.

PUNISHING CATHOLICS

Catholics also suffered as Elizabeth became less lenient. Even as Elizabeth continued to demand Protestantism, Catholics did not leave England entirely. To the contrary, they enjoyed a resurgence in their faith, and the number of people practicing Catholicism grew in the 1570s. They practiced their faith secretly and out in the open. Many Catholics started refusing to conform

Parliament under Elizabeth

Although ruled by a monarchy, English citizens did have some government representation in the sixteenth century. They had a parliamentary form of government, with noblemen filling the ranks of the House of Lords and well-to-do commoners, or people without noble titles, elected to sit in the House of Commons.

The economic growth of the sixteenth century created pressure to increase the size and power of the House of Commons, as the country's merchant class became more affluent and demanding. Members of Parliament also became more willing to question the queen. The Puritan members of Parliament were particularly bold. Elizabeth believed Parliament should not meddle in royal matters. But led by outspoken Puritans, Parliament began to assert itself more during her reign.

Elizabeth signed the warrant for the death of Mary Queen of Scots.

to the principles set forth by the Church of England. In response, Elizabeth condoned the torture and execution of Catholic leaders. And she would allow these practices for the rest of her life, though she would defend herself, explaining she was punishing acts of defiance against the government and the crown and not just religious beliefs.

In 1586, Elizabeth learned of another plot to assassinate her and put Mary Queen of Scots on the throne. It was then that Elizabeth realized she had to take drastic action against Mary or her rival would always remain a threat to her rule, even when imprisoned. Elizabeth signed a warrant for Mary's execution on February 1, 1587. Mary was beheaded seven days later, on February 8.

A Clear Victory

In the late 1580s, Elizabeth had a new threat to contend with—the Spanish Armada, a fleet of warships. In 1588, the Spanish Armada was reported to be anchored in Lisbon, Portugal's capital. More than 100 ships were ready for war, and their sights were set on England. The Spanish Armada was to crush the English navy and deliver Spanish troops to England. Spain intended to put an end to English involvement in the Spanish-controlled Netherlands, which was also experiencing religious fights between Catholics and Protestants. Spain also wanted to end privateering by English captains. Privateering was when government-funded ships attacked enemy ships and stole their supplies. On more than one occasion, the English adventurer Sir Francis Drake had taken treasure and supplies from Spanish ships during raids, including one in 1587 in the harbor of Cadiz, Spain.

England readied itself for war. The queen commanded her lords to muster troops, and the English navy prepared for battle. Elizabeth imprisoned some people thought to be sympathetic to the Spanish, especially Catholics, so they could not aid the Spanish

---

Elizabeth's Tilbury Speech

In August 1588, Elizabeth gave a speech to English troops in Tilbury before they battled the Spanish. Though there are different accounts of her speech, one version contains the following:

My loving people, we have been persuaded by some, that are careful for our safety, to take heed how we commit ourselves to armed multitudes, for fear of treachery; but I assure you, I do not desire to live to distrust my faithful and loving people. Let tyrants fear; I have so behaved myself that, under God, I have placed my chiefest strength and safeguard in the loyal hearts and good will of my subjects.

And therefore I am come amongst you, at this time, not for my recreation and disport, but being resolved, in the midst and heat of the battle, to live or die amongst you all; and to lay down, for my God, and for my kingdom, and for my people, my honor and my blood, even in dust. I know I have but a body of a weak and feeble woman; but I have the heart of a king, and a king of England, too.[3]

if they did invade. Elizabeth made Dudley the commander of Camp Royal at Tilbury. The queen visited the camp in August 1588, giving an inspirational speech that marks a highlight in her long reign.

The English won a quick victory against the Spanish on August 9, 1588. Additionally, much of the Spanish Armada was destroyed in a storm as the ships retreated from battle. With this victory, England put an end to the great Spanish threat, at least for the time being. England and Spain remained enemies, but the English victory over the Spanish Armada is still considered one of the greatest victories in British history.

CONSPIRACIES CONTINUE

Despite these victories, Elizabeth remained vulnerable to attack all her life. King Philip of Spain sent assassins after Elizabeth until he died in 1598. A few made it into the

Francis Drake the Explorer

The seafaring exploits of Sir Francis Drake made him a hero in England. He became famous in 1567 after serving as commander of a ship in a squadron that defied prohibitions against trading to the Spanish. Most of the ships were destroyed as punishment, so Drake turned to plundering Spanish ships and settlements during the early 1570s. In 1577, he set off on a journey that would take him around the world over the next few years. He returned to England laden with Spanish loot in 1580. Elizabeth made him a knight in 1581.

queen's private chambers before guards stopped them. One of her court favorites, Robert Devereux, Earl of Essex, also plotted against her. Devereux, who was Dudley's stepson, planned to seize the court and the Tower of London and then lead Londoners in rebellion. But the queen learned of his plot and had Devereux arrested and executed.

England battled the Spanish Armada in 1588.

*To commemorate the English victory over the Spanish Armada,
Elizabeth had several portraits done.*

THE QUEEN IS DEAD

The last decade of Elizabeth's reign
saw some of the era's most impressive
achievements, including global exploration, New
World colonization, and an English literature boom.
The sun was rising on what would become the British

Empire. But it was clearly setting on Elizabeth. "There are more that look, as it is said, to the rising than to the setting sun," Elizabeth once said.[1]

THE AGING QUEEN

As she aged, Elizabeth lost her beauty. Her long face became thin, gaunt, and lined with wrinkles. Her cheeks were sunken in. Her teeth were black or missing; foreign ambassadors said this made her difficult to understand. She ate very little, possibly because her blackened teeth hurt when she chewed. She was often disheveled and unkempt. When she did wear makeup, it was heavily applied to her face and much of her upper torso to try to hide her age. She wore wigs and jeweled gowns. Historians believe she used these to dazzle visitors and distract them from the obvious signs of her age.

Elizabeth remained engaged in matters of state throughout her senior years, and she returned to reading the classic texts of the ancient world that she had always enjoyed. However, her behavior became

Elizabeth's Motto

Elizabeth adopted a personal motto: *Semper eadem*. This is Latin for "always the same." The motto can be seen on the coat of arms used by Elizabeth. Although chosen early in her life, the motto is seen by some as an important summary of the stability she brought to the monarchy during her long reign as well as the consistency of her approach to ruling.

more erratic as she grew older. She suffered bouts
of depression and would cry or stare blankly. She
stamped her feet in rage upon hearing bad news.
She kept a rusty sword with her, sometimes stabbing
at the heavy curtains in her chambers. Elizabeth's
advisers and courtiers knew she was dying, yet she
would not name a successor.

Elizabeth's Golden Speech

On November 30, 1601, Elizabeth prepared
to address Parliament. She was expected to
speak about routine matters of government, but
instead informed the gathered members that
it would be her last Parliament. The speech,
which came to be called her Golden Speech,
was her farewell. In part, she said,

*My heart never was set on worldly goods,
but only for my subjects' good. What you
bestow on me, I will not hoard it up, but
receive it to bestow on you again. . . .
There will never queen sit in my seat with
more zeal to my country, care to my subjects, and that will sooner with willingness
venture her life for your good and safety,
than myself. For it is not my desire to live
nor reign longer than my life and reign
shall be for your good. And though you
have had and may have many princes
more mighty and wise sitting in this seat,
yet you never had or shall have any that
will be more careful and loving.*[2]

THE COUNTRY STRUGGLES

England had
also fallen on
hard times after
celebrating its
victory over the
Spanish Armada in
1588. The country
had entered into an
ongoing war with
Spain, and the costs
of that war brought
financial hardship
to the queen's
subjects. The
country suffered

failed harvests, famine, and epidemics. At the same time, the English were paying high taxes. Elizabeth fell from many of her subjects' favor during this time.

In addition, the court was becoming more and more corrupt, with rampant bribery and greed. It was important for Elizabeth to name England's next ruler, so there would be someone to lead the people through these challenges. Also, the old question remained of whether the next ruler would be Protestant or Catholic. But Elizabeth would not name a successor.

A Quiet End

Sick and suffering, Elizabeth started having trouble swallowing in early March 1603. Some historians believe she had ulcers in her throat due to influenza or tonsillitis. Sir Robert Carey visited her around this time. He reported on her health and state of mind:

> *I found her in one of her withdrawing chambers, sitting low upon her cushions. She called me to her; I kissed her hand, and told her, it was my chiefest happiness to see her in safety and in health, which I wished might long continue.*

She took me by the hand, and wrung it hard; and she said
"No, Robin, I am not well!" and then discoursed with me of
her indisposition, and that her heart had been sad and heavy
for ten or twelve days.[3]

Elizabeth lost the ability to speak on March 21.
Two days later, she took to her bed. William Whitgift,
the archbishop of Canterbury, stayed with her to
pray. Elizabeth eventually fell asleep. Elizabeth quietly
died sometime in the early morning
hours of March 24 while she slept.
She was 69 years old.

KING JAMES I OF ENGLAND

Elizabeth had never publicly
named her successor. She refused to
do so even as she was dying. However,
she had apparently arranged with
her trusted adviser Sir Robert Cecil,
son of William Cecil, for James VI
of Scotland, the son of Mary Queen
of Scots and a Protestant, to become
the next ruler of England. Even
before Elizabeth's death, Robert had
discussed the possibility with James.

Immortalized in Verse

Elizabeth touched nearly all aspects of English life during her reign. That included poetry and verse. One of the most telling examples is the epic poem *The Faerie Queene,* a 1596 work by Edmund Spenser. Spenser used the poem to celebrate Elizabeth's royal Tudor family, and he referred to her in the poem as "Gloriana" and "Belphoebe." References to her exist in other works as well, including pieces by William Shakespeare, Ben Jonson, and Sir Walter Raleigh. They sometimes called her Diana, as in the classic goddess of the hunt.

James VI of Scotland became James I of England when he succeeded Elizabeth.

When Elizabeth died, Carey was sent riding north to Edinburgh, Scotland. He was to deliver Elizabeth's coronation ring to James as a token of his claim to the crown of England. Elizabeth was buried in a chapel at Westminster Abbey on April 25.

A Lasting Influence

The Elizabethan era is certainly considered a golden age for England, but Elizabeth also left a number of problems for the monarchs who followed her to the nation's throne. The country was in debt. It still had enemies abroad and at home. England remained vulnerable to civil and religious strife.

Yet, there were significant strides made in political and social life as well as in exploration and commerce. England experienced a flourishing of literature during the time, though Elizabeth did enforce censorship rules. However, most people agree that great gains were made in the areas of art and exploration during Elizabeth's reign. ⌐

Elizabeth's tomb in Westminster Abbey

Elizabeth's reign is sometimes called the Golden Age because of all the advances the country made during that time.

THE QUEEN'S LEGACY

The Elizabethan era suffered from civil strife and fighting over religion. People experienced poverty, the plague, and anxiety over the royal succession. Most people lived a life of subsistence in which they were just barely getting by with food and other necessities. Many lived in bare cottages and had meager diets.

Yet, the era is also known for its progress and periods of prosperity. Despite the periodic rebellions, Elizabeth is credited with unifying her country. England's population underwent significant growth, increasing by about one-third from approximately 3 million people to 4 million during her reign. Although many of Elizabeth's subjects lived in poverty, the members of the upper class enjoyed many luxuries, and there was a growing merchant class that was building its wealth. In addition, she encouraged exploration, which brought new riches into the country and set the stage for England's future as an empire that spanned the globe. Elizabeth also ruled over a period that saw great achievements in literature.

The People's View of Elizabeth

Though England contended with hard times during the last years of Elizabeth's reign, the people looked upon Elizabeth with a special reverence. The queen's subjects showed more than respect and affection for their ruler. Many came to see Elizabeth almost as a quasi-divine ruler, despite some of the unpopular actions she took during her reign.

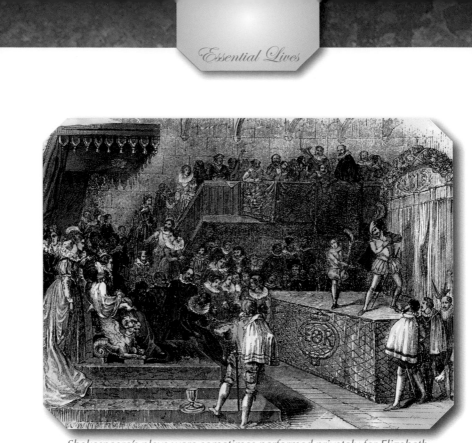

Shakespeare's plays were sometimes performed privately for Elizabeth.

Literary Endeavors

Elizabeth's support of literature came mostly through the patronage system. Elizabeth spent little of her own money supporting the artists and intellects she welcomed into her court. But like other monarchs in that era, she encouraged her courtiers to financially support poets and playwrights. Like other rulers, she favored those artists and writers whose work promoted her own ideas and ideals, such as civil order and obedience.

The literature created during Elizabeth's first decades in power followed a traditional path, as it usually had religious themes and reinforced the religious and social agenda Elizabeth and her court wished to establish. However, the poems and plays from the latter part of Elizabeth's reign showed interest in new subjects and emotions. The literature of that later age address topics ranging from money to love. It also reflects the events happening in England at the time. Some of William Shakespeare's plays mirror the political issues of the era, including rebellion and anxiety over royal succession.

SUPPORTER OF THE ARTS

This flourishing of the arts came from different causes, among them the victorious spirit following the defeat of Spain and the excitement from New World exploration.

A Golden Age

The Elizabethan age is also often referred to as a golden age for England. Although Elizabeth's reign was not without problems, the fact that she ruled for so long and oversaw much progress led to the belief that the era was a particularly significant one in English history.

The queen was well educated, and spoke six other languages, including French, Italian, and Latin. She also enjoyed music and dancing, so it is not surprising that she was a patron of the theater, too. However, she never actually attended the public theatre. Plays were performed for her privately. In fact, Shakespeare's *The Merry Wives of Windsor* was reportedly produced on orders of the queen. And she enjoyed performances of other productions, including Shakespeare's comedy *Love's Labour's Lost*.

A Literate Public

Elizabethan England also saw explosive growth in printed material and education, which were boosted by the increasing prosperity of the merchant class. The upper classes had the means to accumulate enough books to fill personal libraries, though the numerous pamphlets printed during the time were more affordable to those of modest means.

England also saw a dramatic increase in the number of people who could read, including those in middle and lower classes of society. Sixty percent of London's craftsmen and tradesmen were literate in the 1580s.

ELIZABETH'S EXPLORATION

Elizabeth also presided over another of England's significant advancements on the world stage: global exploration. When she became queen, England was poor and wielded much less power than other nations, particularly France and Spain. Yet, Elizabeth and the country's noble families craved the same luxuries rulers and courtiers in other countries enjoyed. This created a demand for goods such as silk and exotic foods, which were being transported to Europe from around the globe. Elizabeth and other English nobles also wanted to make money from this new global trade.

Elizabeth agreed to help pay for expeditions, and she required

Finance and Commerce

Elizabeth had a keen interest in financial matters, both on the personal level and on the national one. She worked with her advisers to make currency reforms to ensure the best economic exchanges for her country.

She carefully watched government spending. Elizabeth brought this same attention to finances to her personal wealth. She worked with her advisers to make sure her lands were as profitable as possible and that she could save money. Elizabeth worried that taxing her citizens would make them dislike her. So, Elizabeth usually borrowed money instead. However, this increased the country's debt.

Her keen sense of financial matters influenced the age of exploration. Commercial interests prompted much of the exploration that happened during Elizabeth's reign, and she was eager for those in her court to financially support merchant interests as a way to advance the English economy.

the men around her to do the same. But Elizabeth did more than fund these overseas ventures. She was always concerned about personal safety and the security of her realm. So, she promoted trade, exploration, and eventually colonization as vital to the interests of a secure and prosperous England.

Elizabeth's perspective helped establish England as a naval power. She sanctioned, or allowed, privateering. Ship owners, for their part, also saw an opportunity to get rich by plundering others' goods, a portion of which went to the queen.

Elizabeth's Adventurers

Sir Francis Drake circumnavigated the globe from 1577 to 1580, making him the first Englishman to achieve the feat. But at the time, the English celebrated him more for showing that Spain was not the only power that could rule the seas. Elizabeth, who had backed Drake on his adventure, was pleased that he had plundered a Spanish treasure ship, the *Cacafuego*, and made off with its cargo of silver and jewels.

At the same time, English adventurers started to explore the New World and claim territory for England. In the 1580s, Sir Walter Raleigh organized the first English expedition aimed at colonizing North America. In 1584, his captains, Philip Amadas and Arthur Barlow, landed on the area that is now North Carolina's Outer Banks. Although initial attempts at colonization there failed, Raleigh's expedition paved the way for England's presence in North America.

With a new century on the horizon, the merchants who owned many of the English ships enjoyed success in their commercial ventures. Rulers were impressed by the English seaman who had defeated Spain in 1588 and greeted them in faraway lands.

BELOVED QUEEN

Elizabeth's appreciation of artist endeavors, education, and exploration helped advance her beloved country. She had set in place the start of what would become the

Naming the New World

Elizabeth's influence can be seen in the United States. The state of Virginia traces its name back to the Virgin Queen, a nickname for Elizabeth. After the expedition organized by explorer Sir Walter Raleigh landed on an island off the coast of what is now North Carolina in 1584, Raleigh asked Elizabeth if she would allow him to name the new land for her. The name Virginia was originally given to the entire Eastern Seaboard, from what is now Newfoundland in Canada to Florida in the southern United States.

British Empire. Arguably the best known female leader in history, Queen Elizabeth I is also perhaps one of the most successful monarchs in English history. ⌒

Queen Elizabeth I was remembered fondly after her death.

TIMELINE

early 1530s	1533	1536
Henry breaks from the Catholic Church, establishing Protestantism as the Church of England in November.	Anne Boleyn, the second wife of Henry VIII, gives birth to Elizabeth on September 7.	Boleyn is beheaded on May 19.

1549	1553	1553
Thomas Seymour is beheaded for his part in a plot against King Edward VI on March 20.	King Edward VI dies on July 6.	The coronation of Mary takes place at Westminster Abbey on October 1.

1537	1544	1547
Elizabeth's half brother, Edward, is born in October and becomes next in line for the throne.	Henry and Parliament officially establish the order of succession. Elizabeth is third in line for the throne.	Henry dies on January 28.

1554	1558	1559
Elizabeth is taken to the Tower of London in January. She stays there for two months.	On November 17, Elizabeth becomes queen at age 25.	The coronation of Elizabeth I takes place in London on January 15.

TIMELINE

1559

The new English
service is held for
the first time in the
Queen's Chapel
on May 12.

1559

Elizabeth sends
English soldiers to
help the Protestant
Congregation
in Scotland.

1560

Robert Dudley's wife
dies. Controversy
surrounding her
death makes Dudley
unsuitable to
marry Elizabeth.

1579

François, Duke
of Alençon and a
possible husband
for Elizabeth,
arrives in England
on August 17.

1587

Elizabeth signs
the death warrant for
the execution of
Mary Queen of Scots
on February 1.

1587

Mary Queen of Scots
is executed on
February 8.

1562	1563	1570
Elizabeth catches smallpox and nearly dies in October.	John Foxe publishes the first edition of his *Book of Martyrs.*	The pope excommunicates Elizabeth on February 25.

1588	1588	1603
Elizabeth arrives in Tilbury on August 8, rallying English troops there with a rousing speech met with great applause.	England defeats the Spanish Armada on August 9.	Elizabeth dies at Richmond Palace on March 24.

Essential Facts

DATE OF BIRTH

September 7, 1533

PLACE OF BIRTH

Greenwich Palace in London, England

DATE OF DEATH

March 24, 1603

PARENTS

King Henry VIII, Anne Boleyn

EDUCATION

Elizabeth was well educated by tutors.

MARRIAGE

None

CHILDREN

None

CAREER HIGHLIGHTS

In religious decisions, Elizabeth tried to avoid the extremisms of the radical Protestants and the Catholics. In doing this, she managed to unite her kingdom under one religion and maintain a relatively peaceful country. Under Elizabeth's leadership, the English secured a victory over the Spanish Armada in 1588.

SOCIETAL CONTRIBUTION

England made many contributions to literature, art, politics, and exploration during Elizabeth's reign. She was a devoted patron of these endeavors and encouraged her royal court to support them as well.

CONFLICTS

Elizabeth's life was often threatened by those who disagreed with her rule or hoped to have a Catholic ruler. Elizabeth's reputation was occasionally slandered by her own people, making other leaders suspicious and disrespectful of her.

QUOTE

"Be ye assured that I will be as good unto you as ever queen was to her people. . . . Persuade yourselves that for the safety and quietness of you all, I will not spare, if need be, to spend my blood."—*Elizabeth I*

GLOSSARY

ascend
> To rise or advance, as in rank.

bawdy
> Indecent, offensive.

blasphemous
> Disrespectful or offensive, particularly against God.

courtier
> An individual, often of the noble class, associated with a monarch.

depose
> To remove from office.

entourage
> A group of people who follow around another person.

heretic
> A person who holds religious beliefs opposite or different from the accepted beliefs.

illegitimate
> Born to parents who are not married.

liaison
> A relationship.

misnomer
> A wrong or misleading name or description.

muster
> To bring together or assemble.

pious
> Very religious.

quell
> To stop, end, or crush.

resurgence
> To rise or grow again.

reverence
> Deep respect or awe.

sedition
> An act or revolt against the government.

shirk
> To avoid.

sordid
> Dirty, unpleasant.

squabble
> To fight.

succession
> A line of people or things in the order they should appear.

treachery
> A betrayal or act of disloyalty.

treason
> An act against one's own government.

ADDITIONAL RESOURCES

SELECTED BIBLIOGRAPHY

Erickson, Carolly. *The First Elizabeth.* New York: Summit, 1983. Print.

Hibbert, Christopher. *The Virgin Queen: Elizabeth I, Genius of the Golden Age.* Reading, MA: Addison-Wesley, 1991. Print.

Levin, Carole. *The Reign of Elizabeth I.* New York: Palgrave, 2002. Print.

Ridley, Jasper. *Elizabeth I: The Shrewdness of Virtue.* New York: Viking, 1987. Print.

Starkey, David. *Elizabeth: The Struggle for the Throne.* New York: HarperCollins, 2001. Print.

Waller, Maureen. *Sovereign Ladies: The Six Reigning Queens of England.* New York: St. Martin's, 2006. Print.

FURTHER READINGS

Adams, Simon. *Elizabeth I: The Outcast Who Became England's Queen.* New York: National Geographic Children's, 2008. Print.

Eding June. *Who Was Queen Elizabeth?* New York: Grosset & Dunlap, 2008. Print.

Fowke, Bob. *The Secret Life of Elizabeth I.* London: Hodder & Stoughton, 2005. Print.

Web Links

To learn more about Elizabeth I, visit ABDO Publishing Company online at **www.abdopublishing.com**. Web sites about Elizabeth I are featured on our Book Links page. These links are routinely monitored and updated to provide the most current information available.

Places to Visit

Hampton Court Palace
East Molesey, Surrey, KT8 9AU, UK
44-(0)20-3166-6000
http://www.hrp.org.uk/hamptoncourtpalace
Hampton Court Palace was one of Elizabeth's many homes. She spent much of her time at this palace and enjoyed walking its well-tended grounds.

Tower of London
London, EC3N 4AB, UK
44-(0)844-482-7777
http://www.hrp.org.uk/toweroflondon
The 1,000-year-old fortress that held monarchs and prisoners is open to the public for tours.

Westminster Abbey
20 Dean's Yard, London SW1P 3PA, UK
44-(0)20-7222-5152
http://www.westminster-abbey.org
Visitors can see the final resting place of British monarchs, including Elizabeth I.

Source Notes

Chapter 1. Elizabeth Takes the Throne

1. David Starkey. *Elizabeth: The Struggle for the Throne*. New York: HarperCollins, 2001. Print. 235.

2. Ibid. 243–244.

3. Christopher Hibbert. *The Virgin Queen: Elizabeth I, Genius of the Golden Age*. Reading, MA: Addison-Wesley, 1991. Print. 48.

4. Ibid. 73.

Chapter 2. The Unintended Monarch

1. David Starkey. *Elizabeth: The Struggle for the Throne*. New York: HarperCollins, 2001. Print. 19.

2. Ibid. 16.

Chapter 3. The Early Years

1. Christopher Hibbert. *The Virgin Queen: The Personal History of Elizabeth I*. New York: Viking, 2010. Print. 158.

2. Alison Weir. *The Life of Elizabeth I*. New York: Ballantine, 1998. Print. 55.

Chapter 4. The Virgin Queen

1. Jasper Ridley. *Elizabeth I: The Shrewdness of Virtue*. New York: Viking, 1987. Print. 82.

2. David Grant Moss. "A Queen for Whose Time? Elizabeth I as Icon for the Twentieth Century." *The Journal of Popular Culture*. 5 Nov. 2006. Print. 811.

3. Christopher Haigh. *Elizabeth I*. New York: Longman, 2000. Print. 20.

Chapter 5. Challenges to Her Rule

1. Jasper Ridley. *Elizabeth I: The Shrewdness of Virtue*. New York: Viking, 1987. Print. 119.

2. Anne Somerset. *Elizabeth I*. New York: Knopf, 1991. Print. 149.

3. Steven W. May, ed. *Queen: Elizabeth I: Selected Works*. New York: Washington Square, 2004. Print. 37.

Chapter 6. Growing Power

1. Joseph Adolphe Petit. *History of Mary Stuart, Queen of Scots*. London: Longmans, Green, & Co., 1874. Print. 176.

2. Christopher Hibbert. *The Virgin Queen: Elizabeth I, Genius of the Golden Age*. Reading, MA: Addison-Wesley, 1991. Print. 77.

Source Notes Continued

Chapter 7. Conflict at Home and Abroad

1. Carolly Erickson. *The First Elizabeth*. New York: Summit, 1983. Print. 307.

2. Ibid. 309.

3. Diane Ravitch and Michael Ravitch. *The English Reader: What Every Literate Person Needs to Know*. Oxford, England: Oxford UP, 2006. Print. 3–4.

Chapter 8. The Queen Is Dead

1. Leanda de Lisle. *After Elizabeth: The Rise of James of Scotland and the Struggle for the Throne of England*. New York: Ballantine, 2005. Print. 17.

2. Maureen Waller. *Sovereign Ladies: The Six Reigning Queens of England*. New York: St. Martin's, 2006. Print. 244.

3. John Dover Wilson, Ed. *Life in Shakespeare's England: A Book of Elizabethan Prose*. London: Cambridge UP, 1913. Print. 203.

Chapter 9. The Queen's Legacy

None.

INDEX

INDEX CONTINUED

ABOUT THE AUTHOR

Mary K. Pratt is a freelance journalist based in Massachusetts. She writes for a variety of publications, including newspapers, magazines, and trade journals. She has won several awards for feature and news writing.

PHOTO CREDITS